Cherished Castles
Amidst the Clouds

Cherished Castles Amidst the Clouds

Stories and Poems

Irene Kay

VANTAGE PRESS
New York

Illustrations by Tanya Stewart

Cover design by Susan Thomas

FIRST EDITION

Published by Vantage Press, Inc.
516 West 34th Street, New York, New York 10001

Manufactured in the United States of America
ISBN: 0-533-14362-4

0 9 8 7 6 5 4 3 2 1

To all who dare to wish and dream, such as me.

Contents

Cherished Castles
Amidst the Clouds

1

A Field of White Daisies

I am standing in a field of white daisies, a field that stretches for miles and miles. The white daisies outnumber the bright green blades of grass, and the field appears, to my eyes, to be covered with a soft velvet blanket of snow.

However, the afternoon summer sun shines and shimmers and cleverly warms my face, reminding me that the bitterness of the cold winter has, for now, lost its place.

A gentle gust of summer wind purposely brushes against my hair. The wind then teases and flutters the petals of the white daisies to the movement of a delightful symphony composed of flower-fragrant warm air.

The good-natured wind blows and boasts of a promise of happiness for all who dare to wish and dream.

The wind swirls and dances around me, trying its very best to lure me into playing the happiness game.

As I anxiously oblige to the coaxing of the wind, my heart suddenly feels quite free; free from the burdens of everyday life. The refreshed joyous

thumps of my heart almost speak aloud. My smile turns into laughter, making the wind feel proud.

The satisfied wind, having accomplished the task at hand, stands still for just a brief moment and lovingly whispers in my ear, "Enjoy yourself, and be of good cheer, for the sweetness of the warm summer, for now, is here."

2

The Curious Owl

White silken swans float freely, guided by the light of the moon, on a shallow pond; crystal clear.

The reflection of the silvery moon on the surface of the casually rippled water appears to be broken like a shattered antiquated mirror.

A fluffy, chubby, wide-eyed owl, perched in a high nearby treetop, calls out, "Who, who?" His inquiring voice drifts and tumbles softly, methodically, on the misty cloud of haze that hovers above the pond.

As the sound from the owl's query cascades down, on this warm summer's eve, and mingles with the cool dampness in the surrounding sleeping dark dense forest, the peacefulness of the night happily accepts and possesses the blissful hauntingly celestial rhapsody.

The owl waits for an answer, patiently, but no one of any importance responds. The only voices that acknowledge him are the high-pitched shrill sounds of a few little black crickets squeaking in the distance and the utterings of several plump pond frogs, lounging lazily on lily pads, as they murmur their nightly ritual. The frogs' songs sound

similar to an old worn-out accordion groaning, now and again, in a raspy, scratchy voice.

The swans continue to glide back and forth, confidently, on the pond; their heads held high, their smooth, feathered bodies round, their webbed feet paddling slowly, treading the cool refreshing water. They know that they have nothing to fear, for there are angels watching over them to keep them safe from harm. The owl cannot see the angels, but he curiously calls out again, "Who?" Perhaps he can feel their presence and is only asking who is there, just to be polite.

The angels will not answer him, but he will keep wondering and asking throughout the hours of the night.

When bits of morning twilight begin to reveal the thick plush velvet greenery of the awakening forest, the tired curious owl will nonchalantly fall asleep, his head under his wing; tucked snug and tight.

3

Time

Time is an exciting elusive creature. Time wears the mask of a transparent winsome face and moves at an unwary pace.

Time can reflect kindness in the mirror of life, or time can be intimidating; time can lead you on. Time can hauntingly encircle you, curtsy with compassionate grace, and then, behind your back, snatch the breath and life from you without a whisper of a warning.

However, some people feel that time is an elixir, a cure-all for everything, for time has been known to be quite thoughtful and to ease the pain of past events. Yes, time has cried with us and healed many a broken heart. But, there have been days and nights when time has been rather wicked and playful by tickling one's imagination, causing the past to seem worse than it actually was.

Life will affect you in the way that you, yourself, let time rule, as time can heal or time can make of you, a silly helpless fool.

Fortunately, since time, itself, cannot be heard or seen, this simple flaw in time allows us the adventurous courage, inspiration, and freedom to

try to decide for ourselves when to cry, to love, to hope, to trust, to plan and scheme, and, most important of all, to continue to dream.

4

A Secret

Shh! Listen closely, and I will tell you a well-kept secret.

There are bashful guardian angels, dressed in white velvet and velour, who are secretly disguised as clusters of fluffy heavenly clouds, peering down at our picture-perfect world.

Sometimes a little child of innocence will look up and catch a glimpse of the face of one of these celestial beings smiling down at him. But the child will not take notice as he is busy playing and having great fun, nor will he realize the protective power of the angel's shy loving grin.

As the day continues, the angels will faithfully watch over him until the setting of the pink-colored evening sun.

As nighttime approaches and spreads a welcome blanket of yawns and drowsiness, the guardian angels will descend from their hiding places. They will quietly stand next to the little child's bed. And, as he slumbers, breathes, and

dreams, the angels will gently stroke the silken strands of his hair that have settled on his precious brow, while upon a soft feather pillow he rests his weary head.

5

Precarious Pink

Oh, to be free, to mingle with the clouds, to escape from the worldly crowds!

Today, I am a bright pink helium balloon gliding through the atmosphere. I hear noises below me, and I quickly glance downward. I see children looking up at me. They are shrieking with delight. They are running and stretching out their arms, gleefully pursuing me, hoping that they will be able to grasp my long white string that is dangling down and waving about. But I, being a frivolous showoff, gloat and float up higher and higher, far, far above the treetops. I bob and flit about aimlessly. The children are amused and delighted with my fool-hearted antics.

I am conceited, and I am so involved with my own thoughts and aspirations that, suddenly, carelessly, I bump right into the very hot sun. And, "pop!" This is the end of my freedom and of my fun. My mishap is my very own fault; no one else is to blame, not even the sun. My self-made ego is deflated. My heart is broken. My enthusiasm for fun and freedom is gone forever. My pink balloon

pieces flutter down, down to the ground, landing here and there.

The children dance and twirl around as they step and stomp and tramp on my many scattered, bright pink pieces.

Very shortly, the children become bored with the game. They all saunter off together on their way to find a new exciting game to play. They leave me there, all alone, dusty and dirty, tattered and torn.

Now I realize, too late, of course, that I should have been more appreciative, when at the toy store I was born, of my new life and my new fanciful round balloon form.

Outside the toy store, the young child who had proudly clutched the end of my string in his chubby little hand had accidentally let go of the string, oops!

At once, a powerful uplifting feeling caressed me as I began to move toward the blue sky; a surge of energy went through me as up, up, I went.

The little child screeched and pointed toward the sky; tears filled his eyes and, aloud, he cried. His mother looked up and sighed; I was already beyond her reach.

I showed them no sympathy. I didn't care, for at that moment, total freedom was my prize! I felt a desperate devilish desire to take advantage of the situation, and I found transportation on the nearest gust of wind. Far away I flew, not knowing and not caring as to where I was going, or as to what I would do when I got there, or as to what I would end up to be.

Take heed, there is a valuable lesson here to be learned: Be careful and cautious what you desire and what you decide to do, for you only have one precious life to live and one slim chance to be you.

6

A Butterfly

Today, I saw a beautiful butterfly with velvet wings of the deepest color of brown tinged and trimmed with streaks and specks of glistening gold. She was resting on a rock in the soothing radiant rays of the warm sun; her wings so still, she did hold.

When I moved toward her, she quickly flew away. I did not mean to frighten her. I wanted her to stay. For you see, I wondered if the butterfly knew where the angels live. I needed to ask her, if a favor the angels would give.

Sometimes my heart is lonely and in a terrible state of dismay. I thought that the angels might be able to teach me how to understand any downhearted, unfortunate feelings that often occur unexpectedly.

Then I could be truly happy on any old worldly troublesome day.

7

The Lady

I know of a lady so fair who dares to wear garlands of fresh fragrant flowers laced in her long-flowing brown hair.

All through the night she walks slowly, her chin in the air, her eager eyes anxiously drinking in the humble heavenly beauty of the moon and the many stars.

While playful dancing moonbeams caress her silhouette, bashful bits of sparkling dust, fallen from the glimmering stars, cautiously settle in her hair as she travels through the galaxy, far.

Tomorrow, when the lady awakens, she will find that the pockets of her pinafore are filled with tiny precious tidbits of glowing stardust that had gracefully cascaded down from her hair.

The lady I speak of could possibly be me, for I have plotted and schemed and learned to dream of pleasant uninhibited scenes. Nightmares have become old-fashioned, completely out of style.

And, as the dark night begins to fade and surrender to the coaxing of the awakening twilight, and the stars of the vast galaxy begin to lose their glimmer and their glow, I try my very best to think

of the coming bright sun-filled day as being a warm tasty sweet piece of pie, nutritious to the spirit, the mind, and the body; yes, most definitely worthwhile.

8

Candy Castles

If I could fly, ever so high, above the earthly mountain peaks, I would be able to see far beyond my reach. I would probably bump my head on the moon, but it wouldn't bother me, for the quaint old moon has been known to sing to the twinkling stars and to caution and scold the adventurous comets, and, on some occasions, to offer endearing sympathy.

If I could fly up that high into the celestial sky, perchance I would linger and dwell in one of the many enchanting candy castles made of the sweetest sugars of heaven and erected on large fluffy white clouds by merrymaking cherubim.

The cherubim, being pure of heart, work and rest and frolic whenever they please, anywhere, at any time, in the vast galaxy.

Rambunctious vines of ruby red roses anxiously and harmoniously climb and cling tightly onto the outer walls of the candy castles.

The roses not only help to impose a surreal picturesque scene, but they also create a fragrant realm that entices you to come closer and coaxes you to stay for a while.

And, of course, there is always plenty of area left on each cloud that upholds a candy castle for several mythical unicorns (upon which only the cherubim are allowed to ride) to gallop and romp and play, every day.

If I could actually fly up that high, an angel I would surely be, for only then would I have such glorious, elegant, strong wings made of faith, wisdom, peace, and beauty for all the world below to see.

9

The Beginning of the End

One quiet peaceful afternoon, I saw the graceful figure of a lovely, lacy paper angel fluttering in the breeze. Then, a kind and gentle breath of wind whispered in my ear, "There are streaks of silver in your hair."

I knew at that moment that my time to go to Heaven must be near.

The paper angel flew away on the shoulders of the wind, and I stood there wondering when my earthly life would come to an end.

When I die, I am quite sure that I will not be alone; so, therefore, I am not afraid. I feel that I will be happy and privileged to join in the celebrated celestial parade.

I will use my newfound angel wings to help other people. On my wings, I will carry some of the burden of their illnesses and sorrows.

When various persons need to know that the time of their earthly departure is near, I will gladly appear to them as a lacy paper angel; and, if need be, I will let them clutch me in their weary hands to wipe away their timid, heartfelt, salty tears.

10

The Making of Memories

Memories are made of docile dreamy bliss and yesterday's sweet, tasty, summer's kiss.

Tonight, the genteel moon will lull us to sleep. A mist of dew will embrace the stars, causing them to blink and twinkle, amiss.

Tomorrow, the future will come alive, bringing with it the warmth of the bright sun, a sky of sapphire blue, numerous varieties of colorful flowers, plush green grass, and lucky four-leaf clovers. Birds will twitter a good morning song. Our friends will greet us with smiles on their faces. We will have fun and go many places; working, playing, laughing. Kittens will toy with balls of yarn. Dogs will run and tramp through puddles. Little children will grow into adults.

As the days turn into nights and the nights turn into days, the vibrant future will shower us with passionate promises of love, hope, fun, and plenty of time to bask in the sun.

And, each day, as countless seashells continue to wash upon the shores, cherished fond memories will be rekindled, and many more sugar-coated kisses will be mine, and yours.

11

Sleep and Dream

Nighttime dreams are merely shapely shadows dancing on the walls; some are rather short and curt and some are long and tall. Some have friendly jovial faces with smiles a yard long, but some are mean and ugly, causing anguish for us all.

Even though nightmares can create fear and anxiety, pleasant dreams, on the other hand, can be just our cup of tea!

So, go to bed and sleep and dream; do not be afraid. For when the morning sun begins to brighten up your room and you awaken from your sleep, your nighttime dreams, be they bad or good, will quickly cower, and into the cracks of the walls they will hastily seep.

12

Guardian Angels

Adoring angels of the celestial world, spread your wings and fly! Swoop, glide; when you become tired, on a plush white cloud, rest and ride.

Look down at the world where the people live and, without hesitation, your grace, do give.

Watch over our babies, our middle-aged, and our old. For every soul on earth is worth much more than puddles and buckets of the purest melted-down gold.

Here in this world, we have vast amounts of red rubies that glow, crystal-clear diamonds that bedazzle, and glimmering emeralds that are as green as the grass. But these shiny gems are just pretty rocks and are merely superficial toys to hold.

As you can see, from your heavenly home above, the many people who live in this world have individual worries, feelings, problems, and concerns.

Every person here is as different as can be; therefore, all of the people in this world need your love, protection, and compassion, the same as me.

13

A Horse with Wings

One night, I awoke to a curious noise. I sat up in bed and drowsily gazed toward the open window. There, I saw a proud stout white horse with elegant wings, peering in at me.

Seeing me stir, the handsome horse became frightened. He snorted, turned, and fled the scene.

Excitement quickly brushed away my drowsiness. I threw back the bed covers and hurried to the window.

I saw the horse's lofty figure bathed in moonlight as he galloped hastily into the distance. Each click of his hooves upon the cobblestones raised sparks of gold that leaped and flashed and flickered.

As the horse bolted from my view, I saw glints of golden lights appear above the houses and the trees. The fluttering lights were the effects of his hooves pounding on the hard pavement as he traveled through the town.

The farther away he trod, the more dark and dense the night horizon became.

I stood there quietly at the window. I felt confused and puzzled by what I had just witnessed.

As I gently rubbed my eyes, I wondered, *Did I just awaken from an imaginary storybook dream?*

Suddenly, I caught sight of the horse with his wings full-spread, flying high above the buildings and the treetops. Fortunately, for me, the bright round silvery moon had, for an awesome moment, lovingly provided a brilliant picturesque background for the horse's magnificent silhouette. Passing the moon, the horse disappeared into the night.

Left breathlessly behind, my heart thumping irregularly, I knew that I wanted desperately to have gone along with him.

I went back to bed with hope in my heart that one night, soon, that beautiful horse with wings of strength and ability would return to me and let me ride upon his sturdy back, so that I could see the world, from above, in all its finery.

My amazing horse and I would leap across the wide salty blue-green oceans, survey the valleys and the hills, and then take some time to explore the Milky Way Galaxy.

Perhaps we would chase a comet or two. Or, maybe, we would take a walk on the sandy surface of the moon.

We would circle around the planet Mars and say hello to the planet Jupiter.

We would pass by the planet Venus, on the way back home to Earth, and, to our surprise, all of the friendly shiny stars in the galaxy would graciously wink and blink a goodnight kiss to us.